A Friend in Need

FREDDIE REED

In 1985 The Dogs' Home, Battersea, will have been providing care and shelter for the stray dogs (and cats) of London for 125 years. In *A Friend in Need* Freddie Reed, one of Britain's leading photo-journalists, has collected the best of the photographs he has taken at Battersea over many years.

In over sixty superb pictures, Mr Reed presents a portrait of daily life at Battersea, introduces us to many of the characters among the inmates (like Blackie, the dog that grew so attached to his keeper that he kept coming back) and captures those special moments that occur there so often – the joy of a child reunited with a lost dog; the wonder on the face of a small boy meeting his new pet for the first time; the beseeching gaze of a mongrel wanting someone to want him.

Poignant, moving and sometimes heart-rending, *A Friend in Need* is a book for animal-lovers of all ages.

FREDDIE REED, MBE, worked for fifty-one years on the *Daily Mirror*. Starting as a messenger boy, he bought his first camera for twelve shillings and sixpence and studied photography at night school. For many years the *Mirror*'s chief photographer, he has covered wars, earthquakes, and over 64 royal tours and state visits all around the world, winning many awards for his work. His photographs in *A Friend in Need* are the result of over sixty visits to the Dogs' Home.

ERRATUM

The picture on pages 72 and 73 has been incorrectly numbered 6. It should be no. 1.

D1477208

A Friend in Need

A Portrait of Battersea Dogs' Home

FREDDIE REED

Collins

8 Grafton Street, London W1
1985

William Collins Sons & Co Ltd
London . Glasgow . Sydney . Auckland
Toronto . Johannesburg

The photograph on page 19 is reproduced by
permission of the BBC Hulton Picture Library,
the engraving on pages 24–5 by permission of
the *Illustrated London News* Picture Library,
and the photograph of 'Bootsie' by permission
of the *Daily Mirror*. Grateful thanks to
Gerda Massey for her work on the Introduction.

BRITISH LIBRARY CATALOGUING IN PUBLICATION DATA

Reed, Freddie
A friend in need: a portrait of Battersea
Dogs' Home.
1. Battersea Dogs' Home
I. Title
636.7′01′0942166   HV4806.L62B3

ISBN 0-00-217446-4

Made and printed in Great Britain by
Wiilliam Collins Sons & Co. Ltd, Glasgow

To the staff and residents
of Battersea Dogs' Home

Introduction

A DOG'S CHANCE

One of the Dog's Home's fleet of vans has returned with another batch of lost or stray dogs. They are greeted by Dorothy Dockett; the Deputy Superintendent.

What is a dog's chance? Years ago, if you said of someone, 'He hasn't got a dog's chance,' you meant that his prospects were, to say the least, less than hopeful.

Indeed, for many, many thousands of dogs in Britain the situation was hopeless. Disease, ignorance, lack of attention, lack of facilities – let alone cruelty – combined to give them no chance at all.

It was a lucky dog who had good health, a good home, a good owner – and no desire to roam. Such a dog could have his day, and the chances were that he would live his whole life out happily. But for the strays swarming the streets of London and other big cities in Victorian days, the almost certain future was starvation and death.

Today, with modern treatment, better veterinary and other facilities, less poverty, and not least important, enormous publicity, a dog's chance is better than it has ever been before. There is still the harrowing experience of seeing caged strays and disowned dogs, some of which may never find a new home. But, by and large, the story of The Dogs Home Battersea – founded during those Victorian days to care for lost and starving dogs, and celebrating its 125th anniversary in 1985 – is a success story.

Far better that these dogs should be cared for, made fit, fed well – or humanely destroyed if necessary – than that they should be ill, starving and roaming the streets.

While the trains rumble by over the railway arches which form part of the Dog's Home's kennels, two of the kennel maids walk four inmates to the veterinary clinic.

8

Even today, many people don't realize that the vast majority of dogs which reach Battersea are not automatically 'put down' after the seven-day period of grace during which owners may claim them. The home, which legally owns all dogs after that seven-day period, does its utmost to 'save and sell'.

Sick dogs are made well and the public is encouraged to buy. No dog is destroyed unless it is seriously ill or very old. Out of the 20,000 dogs which arrived at Battersea during 1983, no fewer than 15,000 went out again, either claimed by their owners or sold to the public.

'Every dog is given its chance,' says Colonel Henry ('Tod') Sweeney, the Home's Director. 'We do not destroy dogs unless we really have to. We try our very best.'

Partly because of the knowledge that dog diseases are being conquered, partly because of better publicity, and partly because there is less snobbery today, Battersea is becoming more and more popular with the public as the place to find a 'four-footed friend' (there is a cattery too). In fact it seems to be becoming quite a status symbol to have a mongrel from the Home.

'When I first came here ten years ago,' Colonel Sweeney remarks, 'we patted ourselves on the back if we sold 400 dogs a month. Now the figure has doubled to 800. It is becoming extremely popular to have a Battersea dog. People rarely look for pedigree-type dogs today, though we do have some of those; they have come to realize that mongrels can make very good pets.'

One proud owner is television and film star Jeremy Irons. His black and white mongrel is called 'Speed' because he loves to sit in the back of Jeremy's open car, scenting the wind. Jeremy, who opened Battersea's new annexe at Windsor, takes Speed with him everywhere. Now the mongrel is rapidly on his way to becoming a star, too; he has appeared in a number of films with his owner.

Patrick Cargill, another well-known actor, bought a red setter at Battersea; and Frank Muir has a 'scrap of nonsense' which he calls 'Lady Battersea'. He explains: 'You see, she's rather plain. The name gives her a bit of confidence.'

Then there is Betty, the mongrel bitch bought by an Arab oil sheikh and flown by charter plane to his palace in Geneva. For years he sent photographs of his pet back to England. And when he learned that Battersea had opened a new cattery, he decided to try his luck there too. He couldn't come over himself, but he ordered a Rolls-Royce to be sent to Battersea to collect Lady Miaow, take her to the Savoy Hotel for a meal of Dover sole, then on to the airport for the flight to Switzerland.

Battersea's veterinary surgeon, Mr Bill Wadman Taylor, treats a new arrival. He is assisted by his wife, Ruth.

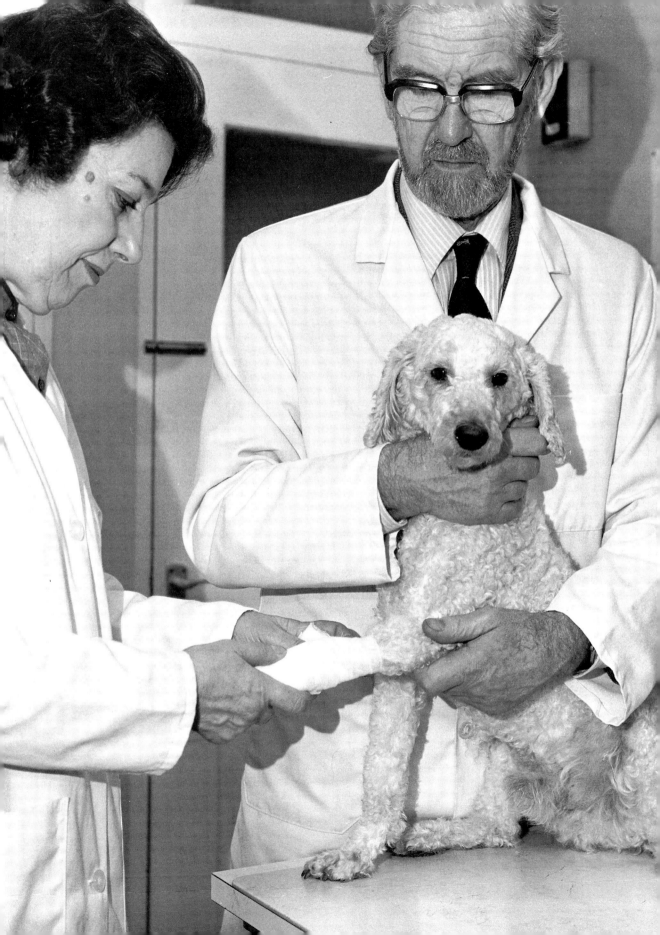

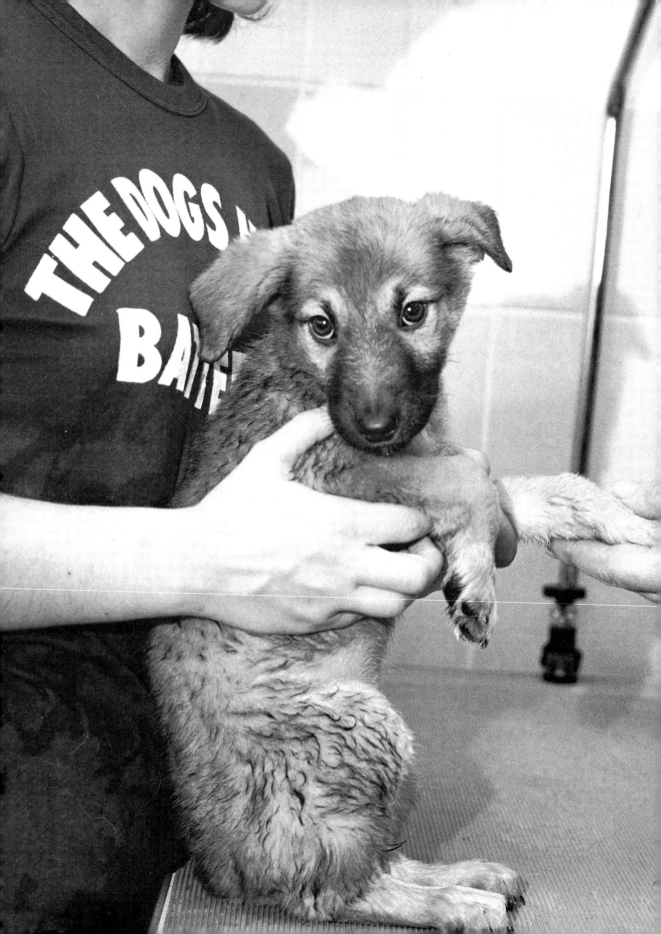

There are so many tales to be told about Battersea, tales both heart-breaking and heart-warming. Tales of owners who go away in tears after searching in vain; tales of joyful reunions and of delighted customers. Many of them appear in this book.

There is the story of Alfie, the mongrel who had reached the end of the line. Seriously ill, he was due to be destroyed – but he sat up and begged, and not one of the attendants had the heart to take Alfie any further towards the death chamber. He was saved, and everyone at Battersea made an enormous effort to cure him. Eventually they succeeded, and Alfie was found a home.

Then there was Blackie, who was sold three times and went to a good home – and three times escaped to turn up again at the gates of Battersea, waiting to be let in. The third time the staff gave in and allowed him to stay – to the delight of the kennel maid whose special charge he had been.

But there is no need to go on ... every picture in this book tells its own story.

Battersea Dog's Home has a staff of fourteen keepers and seventeen kennel maids or kennel men (the majority are maids). All of them, like Blackie's kennel maid, are devoted to their charges, and to their jobs. 'They're special sort of people,' says Colonel Sweeney.

They need to be. The jobs are not well paid – the starting salary is £73 a week – the work is difficult, down-to-earth, in some ways dirty, occasionally even dangerous. Sympathy must there be in plenty, not only for overwrought animals, but for overwrought visitors. And yet Colonel Sweeney has a waiting list of applicants to join the staff ...

Like Blackie, you can't keep some of them away. Take the case of Jack Winterflood, former Deputy Controller. Retired now for four years, he is in his seventies but he still comes regularly to the Home 'in an advisory capacity'; a former RAF Warrant Officer, he could call it 'acting unpaid'.

previous pages and left

As soon as a dog arrives at Battersea, he is given a thorough check-up, first by the Animal Nurse and then by the vet. Every dog gets an injection; some enjoy the luxury of a nice warm bath.

Rich or poor, customers pay the same price – £15 to £50 for a dog, according to breed, around £4 for a cat. There are half rates for pensioners. If for any reason an animal is found not suitable, it may be returned within seven days and the money will be refunded.

Prices are deliberately kept low. The reclaim fee charged to owners, for example, is only £2 per day's stay.

A long-standing member of the office staff at Battersea is Tabby the cat. She arrived at the Home four years ago, and, while waiting for someone to give her a home, took over the 'in' tray of secretary Barbara Graham. And there she has stayed ever since. When Barbara goes home at night, Tabby moves to the kennel maids' rest room.

17

In view of this, it is a remarkable fact that about one-third of Battersea's annual income of well over £700,000 comes directly from reclaim fees and sales. Another third comes from donations and subscriptions made by the public throughout the year. 'People are very generous,' says the Colonel. 'We can't complain. But more money is, of course, always needed.'

Other sources of income include receipts from a contract with the Metropolitan Police, who are obliged, by law, to pay £1.72p a day for the first seven days' lodging of each dog they send in.

Underneath the arches, where the Home is situated on the South Bank of the River Thames, nobody dreams their dreams away (apart, of course, from many of the animals). The Home provides a twenty-four-hour service.

The round begins at 7 a.m. when the first of the day staff arrives, and by 8 a.m. the total complement of over thirty will be on duty.

The first task is to clean out. There are nearly 460 wire-mesh kennels, all equipped with underfloor heating and fibreglass beds. Usually all the kennels are occupied, several by more than one inhabitant. Battersea rarely has fewer than 550 or 600 dogs in residence, so often it is a case of doubling or even trebling up. Each kennel must look spanking-fresh, and smell hygienic when the staff have finished their round.

Every cat must have its day too. In the equally well-appointed cattery (underfloor heating, fibreglass beds), with its new extension, around eighty cages have to be cleaned thoroughly.

Occasionally, the staff will arrive to find that a kennel or cage contains some new arrivals – puppies or kittens which have been born in the hours of darkness. One of the veterinary staff must then be summoned.

Next, feeds must be prepared. Fully grown, healthy dogs are fed with a well-known brand of 'complete dog diet', the compressed, dried lumps which many a private dog-owner finds convenient to use, accompanied of course by plenty of water. This is the main diet, but some tinned food and biscuits may be used too.

A rare picture of Battersea in its earliest days.

For ailing animals, and for motherless puppies and kittens, special diets have to be prepared, and in the kitchens large cauldrons have to be set simmering. Steamed fish and rice, easily digestible, are on the menu for the very sick animal, just as they might be for a poorly human. Other tempting items for the ill are chicken and rabbit.

18

After the dogs have had breakfast, it is time for them to exercise in the yard. The excitement is high as the inmates are let out of their kennels to play together and run about, and often the noise of their barking can be heard above the roar of the trains overhead.

Meanwhile, on the other side of the wire fence, the public must be attended to. It is not unusual to see a queue waiting for the gates to open at 9.30 a.m., and it has been known for people to spend the night outside.

On average, between 200 and 250 people will visit the Home every day, either looking for a lost pet, looking for a new one – or just looking.

There are forms to be filled in – necessary to protect the animals, as well as the public. Owners must give a description of their lost dogs, and state when, where and how they lost them. Even then, the staff will keep a wary eye open to make sure that a lost dog really recognizes someone who claims to be its owner. There may be more questions for the claimant if the dog doesn't know him. The same caution applies with regard to sales. Dogs automatically become the property of the Home after seven days, and the Home is a jealous owner. Healthy dogs are sold – but by no means indiscriminately.

Every would-be purchaser is handed a leaflet quizzing him or her about the care of a dog. Can they afford the upkeep of one (between £4 and £5 a week, plus veterinary fees)? Is their accommodation suitable? Is there an open space nearby where they can exercise their pet every day? Can they make arrangements for the animal to be looked after if they go on holiday? Is there someone at home during the day to look after the animal?

The Home warns that it cannot give a guarantee of perfect health or temperament. But, with great fairness, it gives that guarantee that buyers can get their money back.

All purchasers have to sign a declaration that the animal will not be used for vivisection or other experimental purposes. Last, but not least, the staff are instructed not to sell a dog if they don't like the look of a customer.

And recently the Home introduced an 'after sales' service, to try to ensure, still further, that dogs don't fall into the wrong hands. Two Dog Visitors have been appointed to make random checks at buyers' homes.

Colonel Sweeney, ex Royal Green Jackets, is very protective towards his charges. Rather touchingly, he confesses that he looks on them as if they were his new battalion.

'I was in command of soldiers, and this is not so very much

different,' he says. 'I make my morning inspection, and I try to see to the dogs' welfare, just as I did with my troops.'

What sort of breeds are most popular with the public in 1985? Significantly there is a considerable increase in the demand for guard dogs. 'Alsatians, Dobermann pinschers,' listed the Colonel. 'The big dogs. It's a sign of the times. Some insurance companies claim they're better than any burglar alarm.'

There is still of course a demand for small dogs by flat dwellers, pensioners, and those who can't afford the upkeep of large dogs – but often its a case of the yappier the better. Even a small dog can make enough noise to frighten off an intruder.

During the morning, Battersea's fleet of five red air-conditioned vans has been setting out on its rounds. The drivers cover approximately 180 police stations within a twenty-mile radius of Charing Cross, and each van could bring in around a dozen dogs a day. Sometimes police cars will bring stray dogs directly to the Home. There could be as many as sixty admissions a day.

The pattern has not changed much in recent years. Puppies and kittens are still rescued from dustbins and rubbish tips, dogs are still found roaming the streets – or running pathetically beside a motorway. Just after Christmas, there is the usual significant increase in pets bought as presents for children and turned out once the family has got tired of the new 'toy'. And every summer there is a surge in Battersea's intake caused by heartless people going on holiday. Rather than pay kennel fees, they just dump their pets.

Alongside the returning red vans comes a daily trickle of people bringing in their pets because they can no longer care for them. The cause could be old age, a move to a flat where animals are not allowed, or because they can no longer meet the cost of feeding. The increasing number of broken marriages is another important factor.

Quite often, however, an owner who has brought in a pet will be back the next day to reclaim him – after a sleepless night when he has realized that he just can't bear to be without him.

Every new entrant to the Home is given an 'identity card', a medical check-up, vaccination against all the dog diseases – and a meal.

Many are only too glad to be fed, and to have a good rest. But there are some which will pine and whimper – and a few which will try to bite. Dorothy Dockett, Deputy Superintendent, who has been with the Home for twelve years, is not afraid. 'You get to know how to handle dogs,' she says. 'You have to use a bit of psychology. Its sometimes wise to sit and talk to a dog for quite a long time.' It is very very rare for a member of the staff to have to use a 'dog grasper' – a noose on a long pole. And no one ever hits a dog.

Another, and very important, feature of Battersea is the veterinary clinic, which is busy all day long; but more of that later.

The afternoon wears on, and gradually the day staff goes home. But Battersea never closes. Someone is on duty every night, to make the rounds, to take telephone calls, or Telex messages from Scotland Yard; until the next day dawns, and the round begins again at 7 o'clock.

Battersea today is a very far cry from its beginnings in 1860, when a Mrs Mary Tealby and her friends began caring for strays in the streets of London. They founded the Temporary Home for Lost and Starving Dogs, in Hollingsworth Street, Islington, North London.

Removed to its present site in 1871, the Home was enlarged in 1907, and the older portion was largely rebuilt. Incorporated in 1933, it became a Registered Charity in 1960. In 1975 a large rebuilding project for new kennels, a cattery and a clinic, was completed.

Then came the country annexe at Bell Mead, Windsor, where superb new kennels for whelping bitches and other long-stay dogs are proving 'most satisfactory', according to the Home's annual reports. There is plenty of room for exercise at Bell Mead, with the added pleasure of smelling country smells. Plans are in hand for extending these pleasant premises.

At Battersea itself, extensions have recently been made to the cattery; other new additions are a grooming room, a laundry and a carpenters' shop.

The most important new feature is the veterinary clinic which opened in 1985, having been built at a cost of £125,000. The veterinary side of Battersea's work had been increasing rapidly in recent years, and more room in which to move – and operate – had become an urgent necessity.

The emphasis in the clinic is on medical work – the treatment of distemper, skin diseases, cuts and bruises, etc. – but the staff are also delighted to have their first proper operating theatre, complete with X-ray equipment. Until this was opened, the mending of broken bones, for example, was a somewhat 'kitchen-table' affair.

The Home appointed its first full-time veterinary surgeon, Mr Wadman Taylor, in 1984. Currently he is assisted by his wife,

overleaf

Eight years after Mrs Mary Tealby founded the Temporary Home for Lost and Starving Dogs this picture of some of the Home's inmates appeared in the *Illustrated London News*. The Home was then in Islington, North London.

23

also a qualified vet, and a team of four veterinary nurses, and it is hoped to expand the staff still further.

One matter which takes up more staff time is the new method of destroying dogs by intravenous injection. The old way, using an electric cabinet, was by no means cruel, but intravenous injection is thought to be 'ethically more acceptable'.

The clinic treats up to sixty dogs a day, most of them 'in-patients'. People who have bought dogs at the Home can also make use of its services, and there is a special 'outpatients' clinic free to pensioners for their pets.

Since its foundation in 1860, Battersea has given shelter to well over 2,500,000 dogs. Queen Victoria was the first Patron – or Patroness, as it was called in those days – and it was she who was responsible for extending the three-day limit for keeping dogs to five days. (Under the Dogs Act of 1906 the limit rose to the present seven days.)

Battersea has in its archives a copy of a letter sent to Queen Victoria at Osborne House in the Isle of Wight, by her private secretary, Sir Henry Ponsonby, on 27 December 1885. It reads: 'General Sir Henry Ponsonby humbly begs leave to ask if Your Majesty will be pleased to become Patron of the Lost Dogs Home?' Queen Victoria returned the letter the same day, after scribbling a note across the top: 'Most certainly. No one loves Dogs more than the Queen or wd wish to do more to promote their comfort & happiness. They are man's truest friends.'

The following day Sir Henry wrote to Lord Onslow, President of the Home, informing him of the Queen's acceptance, and adding that Her Majesty would subscribe £10 a year to the Funds of the Institution. The letter went on to say that the Queen had been much interested in all he had told her about the Home after his visit there, and that she thought dogs should be kept for a longer period than only three days.

This suggestion from Her Majesty amounted to a Royal command – and the limit was duly extended.

Royal interest in the Home has continued down the years. The present Queen, whose love of dogs is well-known, has of course been a most popular Patron, and every year in its annual report the Committee has gratefully acknowledged a 'generous donation' from her. Recently it was announced that another Royal animal lover, Prince Michael of Kent, had become President of the Home.

The public has handsomely followed the Queen's example in supporting the Home. Yes, there have been those rich old ladies who have left sums of £50,000 or more in their wills, but they are few and far between. The majority of the money comes in comparatively small amounts from a wide section of the public.

Apart from generous donations, what does Colonel Sweeney want from the public in this 125th anniversary year?

'Take more care of your animals,' he urges. 'If we could reduce the number coming in by one-third, we would be able to find a home for every one – and spend more money on the veterinary side.

'Generally speaking, non-pedigree bitches should be spayed, non-pedigree dogs neutered. It's extraordinary how people are much more reluctant to have this done to their dogs than they are to their cats.

'If only people would be more caring, and not allow their animals to breed indiscriminately, we would be all right. This applies to those who support this Home, as well as those who don't care.'

Colonel Sweeney's remarks are supported by Mr Wadman Taylor in his professional capacity – with the reservation that people should always be careful to consult a good vet. Dogs, for example, could be neutered too young – 'It's not just a black and white case.'

But he is scathing about sentimentalists. 'It's nonsense to suggest neutering is undignified – it's giving animals human attributes. I've known men who wouldn't have their male dogs neutered – as if it were a reflection on them ...

'Much happier the dog sitting by the fireside than going out and getting into fights and developing septic wounds.'

So, fundamentally, layman and expert agree. The message is – take care of your dogs and give them a chance.

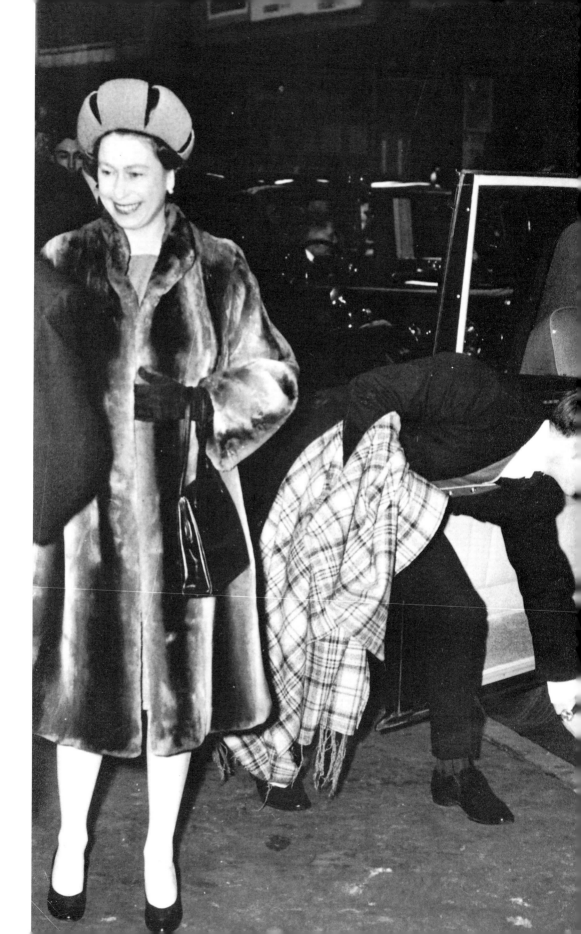

A helping hand

Her Majesty the Queen has
been Patron of the Dogs'
Home for many years and
she takes a keen interest in
the work at Battersea.
Here she is seen arriving
at Kings Cross Station,
accompanied by her pet
corgis. One needed a little
help to get back into
the limousine and
Her Majesty's valet had
to do the necessary.

New arrival

Every day a long line of
pets arrives at the Dogs'
Home. Some are old and
weary; others, like this little
dog, look forward to a long
life in a happy home.

far right

Lost property...
found on the
Barking route

He started by taking a non-
paying ride on a bus on the
North Woolwich to Barking
route. The conductor tried
to put him off, but he just
wouldn't budge and went
on to Upton Park Garage.
As he had no collar, his
next stop was the Lost
Property office, where he
was given a label – 'DOG'.
But you can't stack away a
dog like an umbrella, a hat
or a briefcase, so his
journey ended at Battersea,
waiting for his owner to
claim him.

30

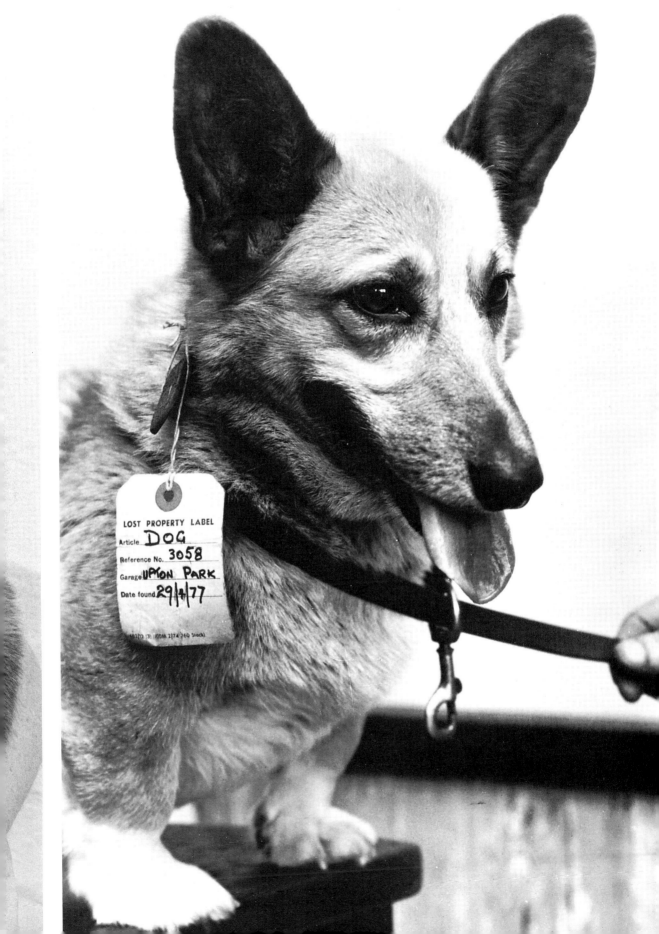

LOST PROPERTY LABEL
Article DOG
Reference No. 3058
Garage UPTON PARK
Date found 29/4/77

Bootsie

In October 1976 this mongrel was found on a platform at Charing Cross Station, guarding his master's shoes. Despite the efforts of staff and police he refused to budge – or to part with the shoes. A member of the Dogs' Home staff managed to coax him away, but the shoes had to go too.

When I took this picture in the kennels at Battersea, he still would not leave the shoes or eat. The publication of the photograph in the *Daily Mirror* brought an astonishing response. Battersea alone received 1,700 letters and calls from people wanting to adopt 'Bootsie', as he had inevitably been christened; hundreds of others contacted the newspaper.

After much deliberation, the Dogs' Home chose a Mrs Webber of Bristol as Bootsie's new owner. She wrote every year, giving them news of the dog, until October 1984 when she sent the sad news of Bootsie's death. 'We have known love, laughter and happiness through Bootsie and his comical antics,' she said. 'We are heartbroken and lost without him.' Mrs Webber sent a donation of £8 – '£1 for every year we were lucky enough to have him ...'

33

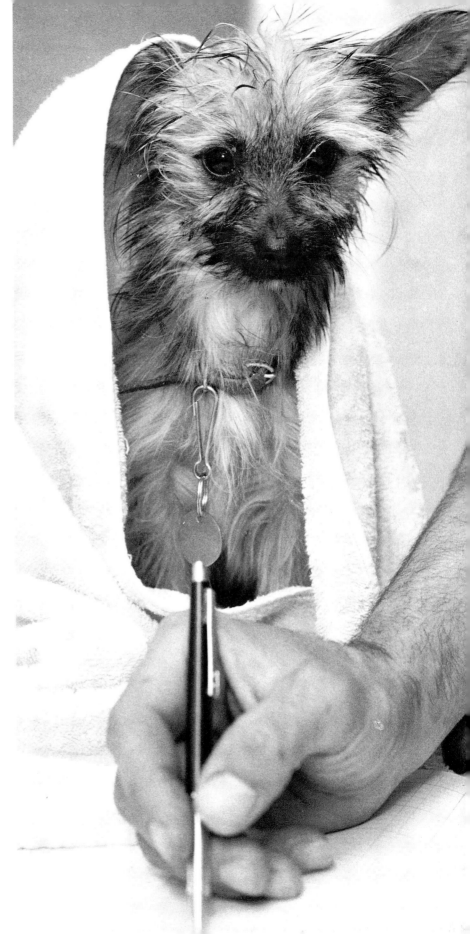

left

Scruff

He is not the smartest of dogs, or the neatest. You could hardly call him handsome. But he has bright eyes, and he's very friendly. At the Dogs' Home he went by the name of Scruff, one of the many dogs of odd shape or size, long-tailed, long-eared, short and fat, waiting for someone to want them, waiting for someone to say, 'Come on, Scruff!' And someone did . . .

right

Damp outlook

Very wet, wandering aimlessly through the London traffic, he was rescued by an animal lover and taken to the local police station. A few hours later a girl from the Dogs' Home arrived to pick him up. After a medical check-up, a bath and a brush-down, he became the latest number in the big book.

Hobo

A ten-year-old Alsatian, he
was found one night tied up
outside the Dogs' Home.
He weighed just twenty-five
pounds and had been badly
scalded by boiling fat.

Loved and spoilt by all
the kennel staff, he found
a super home when he was
well enough to leave. And
when his new owner took
him back for a visit a few
months later, Hobo was
as fit as a fiddle.

36

Checking in

No name . . . not even
a number as yet, a very
young puppy is signed in by
Diane McLelland Taylor.

39

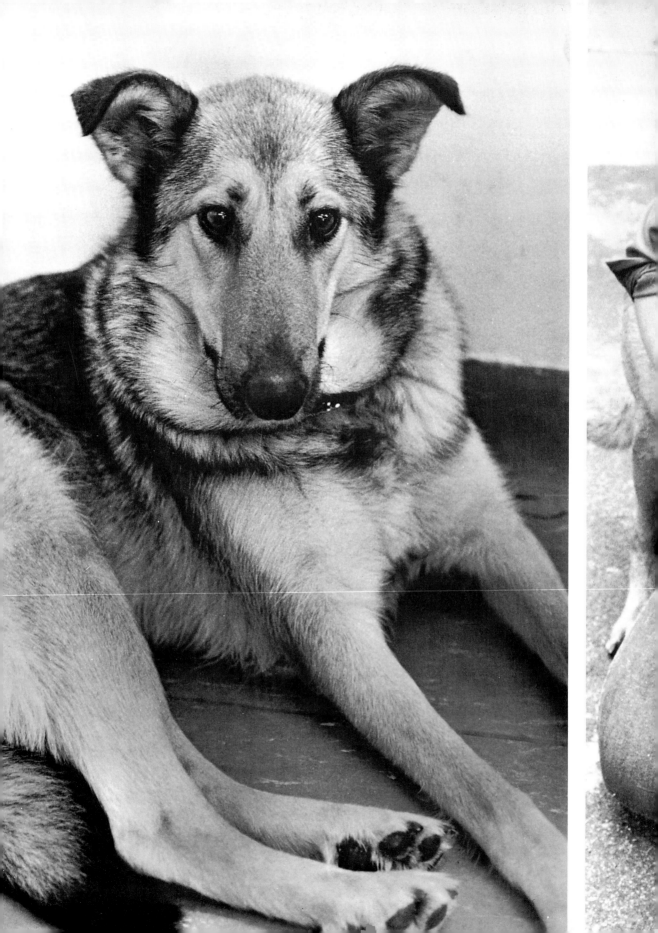

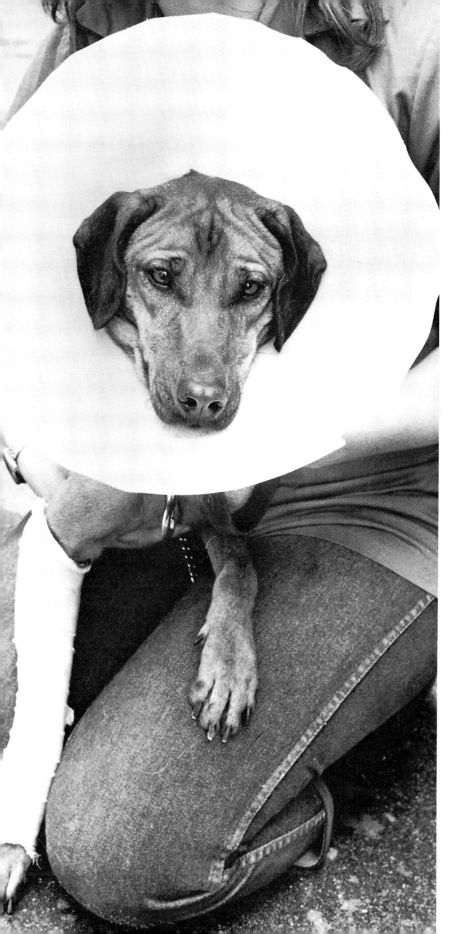

far left

Playing it cool

If you're looking for a new master, it doesn't do to make a fuss. Better to play it cool and let your good looks do the work . . .

left

Dumped

This three-year-old mongrel was pushed out of a car in London's Belgravia. When he arrived at the police station he was found to have a broken leg. The Blue Cross mended his leg and then he was off to Battersea. The huge collar was fitted to prevent him chewing the plaster on his leg.

Safe at last

This labrador had just arrived in Battersea's front hall when Fred Hearne, the yard superintendent, bent down and picked her up. She somehow knew that from now on everything was going to be all right . . .

42

The winners among the lost

Once, some of these greyhounds must have had the cheers of the crowd in their ears as they raced round the track in pursuit of the electric hare... They arrived in ones and twos at Battersea, till – unusually – the Home had fifteen in residence at once. New homes have been found for some, but they keep on coming...

Two's company

Even in the warmth of a kennel at Bell Mead, Battersea's country home at Windsor, it's nice to have a woolly toy for company while you play the waiting game.

overleaf left

Crackers

It was nearly Christmas when this little puppy was found limping along Victoria Embankment. With no collar and no name, he was taken to Battersea. The veterinary surgeon found he had a broken leg and set it in plaster. All he needed now was a name. As their new charge would be spending the festive season at the Home, the girls called him Crackers.

overleaf right

Penny and Tuppence

When this unwanted pair arrived at Battersea within a few minutes of each other, they were given numbers like all the other inmates. But when the new arrivals made friends, the kennel maids decided to name the kitten Tuppence and the puppy Penny.

47

far left

The dog who begged to live

Six years ago this dog was very ill and due to be put down. When he reached the end of the line of dogs waiting to be destroyed, he just sat up and begged . . .

None of the staff had the heart to take him further and, despite the seriousness of his illness, they decided to make a special effort to restore him to health. Eventually they succeeded and he was found a home.

Six years passed and the dog was back in the line. And again he sat up and begged. The staff recognized him and, once again, he cheated death. Now over ten years old, he's been found another home, where he's living happily.

left

Settling down

When the dogs and puppies arrive at Battersea they take a while to settle down in the new environment. This little fellow needed a tiny bit of extra attention from kennel maid Trudy Davies.

far left

Taking his medicine

It was the end of November, the weather was cold and damp, and this puppy really needed some help after being found near Arsenal football ground in North London. He looked so cold that one of the kennel maids fixed him up with an outfit from a discarded doll. Then it was time for his medicine, laced with sugar to help it go down.

left

Scamp joins the party

Picked up in East London, this young puppy arrived at Battersea just in time for Christmas. Named Scamp by the kennel maids, he was the centre of attraction at their Christmas party.

53

2

4

Waiting and hoping

Every day, searching eyes peer through the wire of the cages. Some, like this girl from East London (1) are seeking a lost pet. Others are looking for a new pet – for a good-looking dog, one that is clever and obedient, a dog that is quiet but will make a good guard-dog, but above all for a puppy. Puppies like these two (2) are in short supply, however.
And they all grow up...

Three-year-old Verity Lambert didn't want a puppy, she wanted the wet, bedraggled mongrel bitch she found wandering the streets. But first there was the endless wait to see if the dog would be claimed by her owner. Finally, the day came... and Verity's dream came true (3, 4, 5).

right

Cassidy

When this lovable rascal arrived at Battersea the kennel maids could hardly believe their eyes: he had only three legs. Promptly dubbed Cassidy, he was very healthy and was put up for sale when he wasn't claimed. 'It is extremely rare for us to have a three-legged pet,' said the Superintendent of the Home. 'This one obviously had a very expensive operation, an amputation done very well, and he has overcome the disability well.'

A few weeks later Cassidy was found a new home and is now enjoying life to full ... even with three legs.

right

Just a face

One of the many looking
out . . . at those looking in . . .

62

overleaf

Mother was very clever

These four tiny poodles are lucky to be alive. Their mother walked into the police station at Woodford, East London, and during the night, before the van from the Dogs' Home had arrived, gave birth to four puppies. The mother was ill, and later died, despite all the efforts of the staff at Battersea.

One of the kennel maids took responsibility for the puppies, taking them home with her at night so that they could be fed every hour. When they were four weeks old she fitted them out with jackets and fed them on baby food. They were not in the home for long ... being pretty does help.

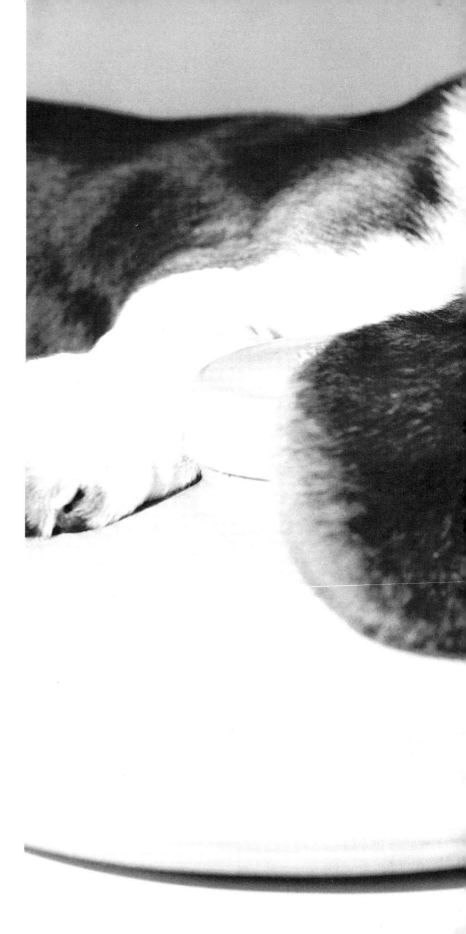

Bertie

It is very rare for a puppy
as young as eight weeks –
and a valuable dog, too –
to be found wandering the
streets of London. But such
was the fate of Bertie the
bassett hound. After a brief
stay in a police station
he arrived at Battersea,
where with the comfort of
a hot-water bottle, some
good food and rest, he
began to enjoy life again.
At least, that's what they
told me: Bertie doesn't
seem quite
so sure . . .

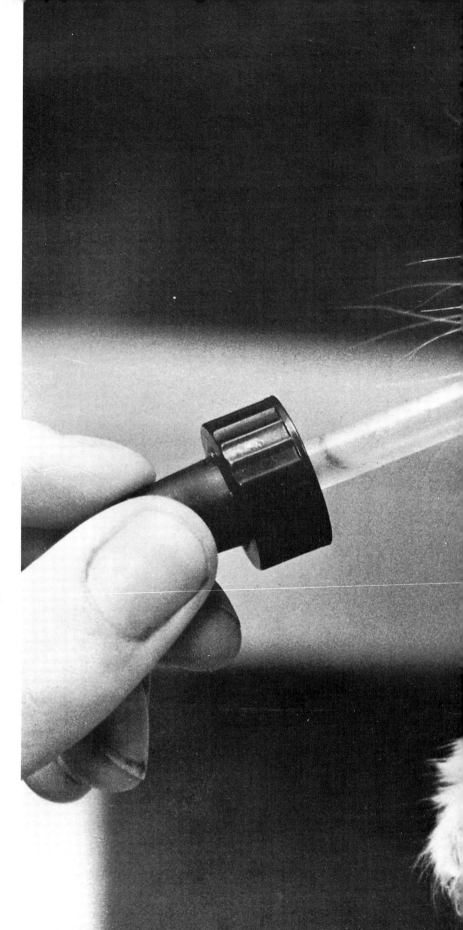

Doctor's orders

A kitten may seem out of place in a dogs' home, but at Battersea they look after many lost or strayed cats.

This one needed special care and attention. Because he was very thin and cold one of the kennel maids knitted him a woollen coat to keep him warm, and the vet prescribed some special medicine...

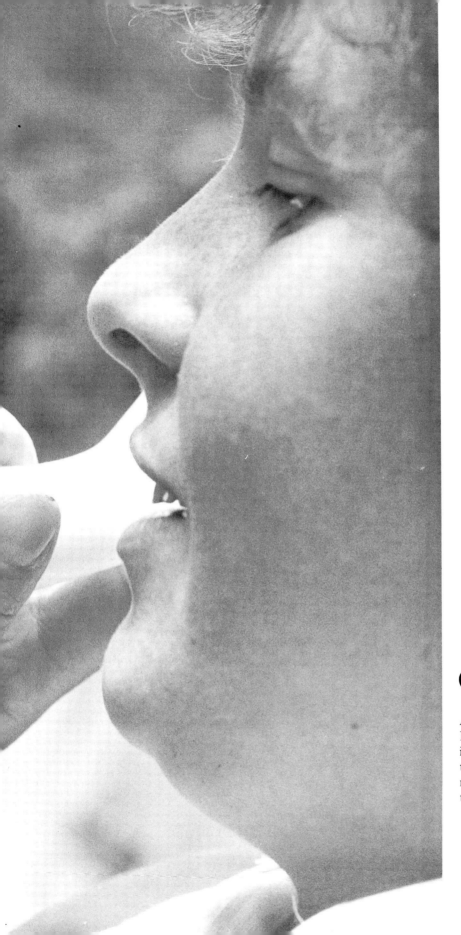

Open wide

At Bell Mead, the Dogs'
Home Battersea looks after
its long-stay inmates like
this tiny puppy. And kennel
maids come from all over
the world to be trained.

71

Star turn

The dogs at Battersea probably see more stars
than the rest of us. At one of the kennel maids'
Christmas lunches, stars like Terry Scott,
Sue Lloyd and Tommy Steele brought their dogs
to meet the inmates. Here (1), Jilly Cooper's
setter Maidstone takes a well-earned rest
after lunch.

Other stars have found their pets at Battersea,
like Liza Goddard and the five-month-old puppy
she calls Gracie (2); Jeremy Irons and Speed (3);
Patrick Cargill and his red setter Harriet (4);
and Pat Coombes and Albert (5), so-called
because he was rescued from the Thames
near Albert Bridge.

Katie Boyle's Bizzie Liz (6) didn't come
from Battersea, but her mistress is often found
there as Katie is a tireless member of the
Home's committee.

First meeting

Two-year-old James
Ducadle meets his new
playmate for the first time.

NOTIC

NG PURCHASER

reminded that while many excellent
. It is impossible for the Commit
ty with regard to them, or to &
atever.

arly understood that they are mos
nstables in the London streets, w
weeks, and brought to the He
own of their antecedents, the
inal Prices are

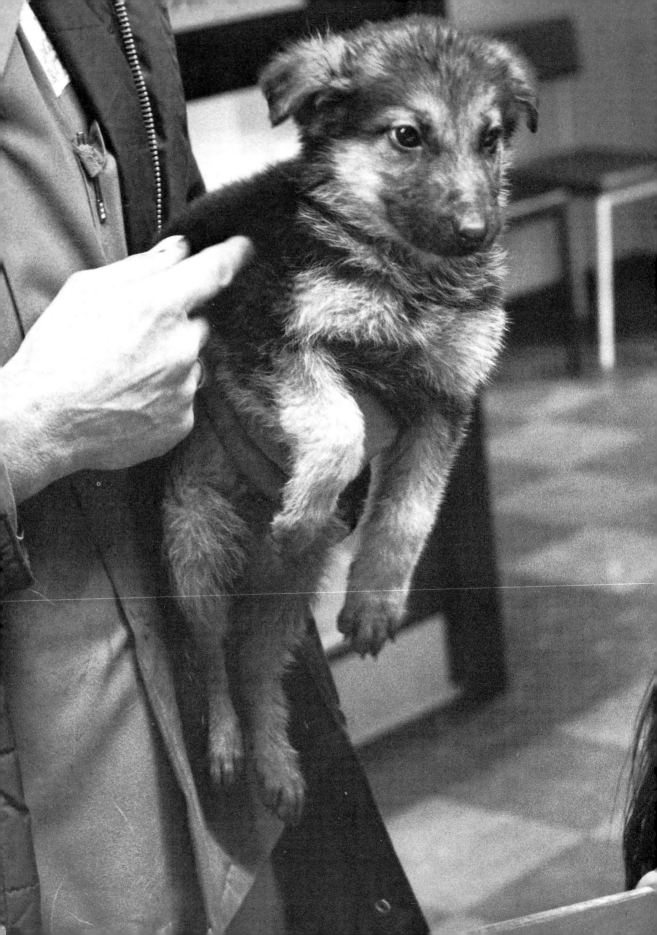

Will they let me have him?

While a keeper holds the dog she has chosen, a little girl waits at the counter. For her this is the longest part of the day. There are so many questions to be answered – the dog's history, his number, whether he is fit, when he was found – and only one to be asked.

83

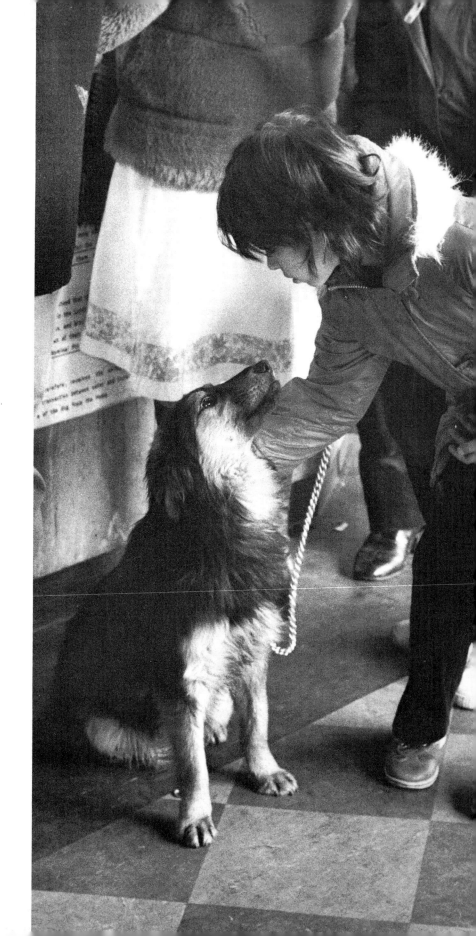

Made for
each other

A lost dog, as yet without
a name, meets his new
owner. Scenes like these
are enacted daily at
the office counter.

84

Worth waiting for

When Paul and Clare Wooley saw this collie behind bars they couldn't take the risk that someone else would get him on the morning that he came up for sale. So they camped out all night outside the Dogs' Home and Ross – as they called him – was theirs.

He's mine

A boy and his dog . . .

Every dog has his day

And for this lucky mongrel that day is today.

Pure joy

Another of those moments that makes everything worthwhile for the staff of the Dogs' Home.

Odd man out

On their rounds of
London's police stations,
the Dogs' Home vans
collect every type of dog.
But it is not very often that
a fully grown St Bernard
finds its way into the legion
of the lost. Just how *do* you
lose a St Bernard?

95

How Leyla fell in love with her nurse

When this cross-bred collie arrived at the Dogs' Home she needed immediate attention for a badly cut mouth. Sue Vickers, the Royal Animal Nursing Auxiliary on duty, thought at first that it would need stitching, but with careful bandaging the bleeding was stopped. After careful nursing, the five-year-old bitch, now named Leyla, was ready to go out into the world again.

A new home was found for her, but as soon as a window was lowered in the car taking her away, Leyla sprang out and went dashing back to Battersea. As soon as the front door was open, she made straight for the surgery and settled down beside Sue.

Another home was found for her, but Leyla pined and was returned to the Dogs' Home. This time she was allowed to stay – and wherever Sue goes, Leyla is with her . . .

Prince

While Prince Charles was
marrying Lady Diana
Spencer at St Paul's
Cathedral, this little dog,
weighing only one pound,
was found abandoned by
a passer-by. She carried him
across London to Battersea,
where the kennel maids had
no difficulty in choosing
his name.

previous pages and right

In custody

Some of the saddest inmates of the Dogs' Home are the pets of people who have been sent to prison. While their owners are in gaol, the dogs are kept behind bars at Battersea or Bell Mead.

Many stay for long periods and their routine is not unlike that of their owners: exercise periods, regular meals and long, empty hours staring through the bars of the kennel. Looking after these dogs day after day, the kennel maids inevitably become attached to them and find it a wrench when they leave. In some cases the girls have adopted a prisoner's dog when the owner has decided he doesn't want him back.

Shane (*right*) was the youngest dog ever to be 'sent to gaol'. He served his time at Bell Mead until his owner relinquished his rights to him and the puppy went to a good home.

102

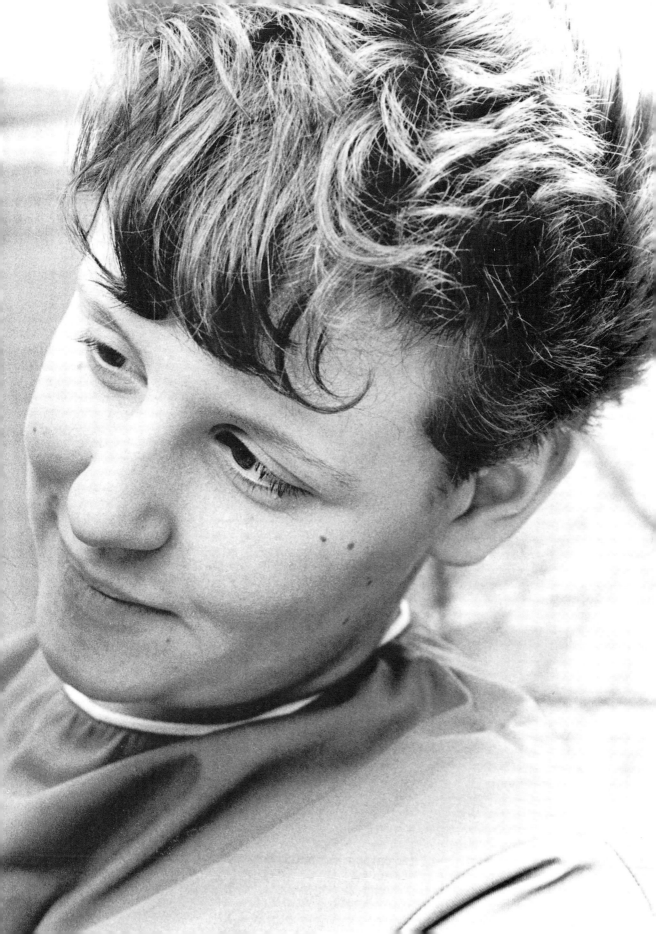

left

Travellers

Dogs travelling on the
famous liner *QEII* go first
class. The ship has its own
kennels, run by staff from
Battersea or Bell Mead,
an exercise deck where the
animals can get their sea
legs, and a special lamp-
post for their convenience.

right

Bill, a twelve-month-old
Staffordshire bull terrier,
left Battersea for America.
His journey by jet, at a fare
of nearly £300, required
special medical check-ups
and all the necessary
certificates.

Blind love

This corgi, receiving a little love and affection from his kennel maid, is blind. But so well developed were his other senses that this was only discovered after a careful veterinary examination.

106

Found

Several days after Sasha
escaped through a hole in
the garden fence and set off
into the world, she is
reunited with her owner.

left and overleaf

A special relationship

He's just another mongrel among the millions that have entered the gates of the Dogs' Home, but Blackie has a special place in the story of Battersea.

Three times he has been sent to a loving family, and each time he has found his way back. At first it was thought that Blackie was a bit of a romantic and was being drawn back to Battersea by the lure of all the female dogs inside. Before his last venture into the outside world he had an operation to quell his loving instincts, and *still* he came back.

The attraction, it seems, was not the lady dogs but June Haynes, the kennel maid who nursed him through severe bronchitis.

The Home's authorities have now relented and Blackie has a permanent place in the doghouse. He has a special resident's kennel, and hand-me-down Harrods coat, and a job as a guard-dog. And last summer the staff had a collection to send June and Blackie for a day at the seaside.

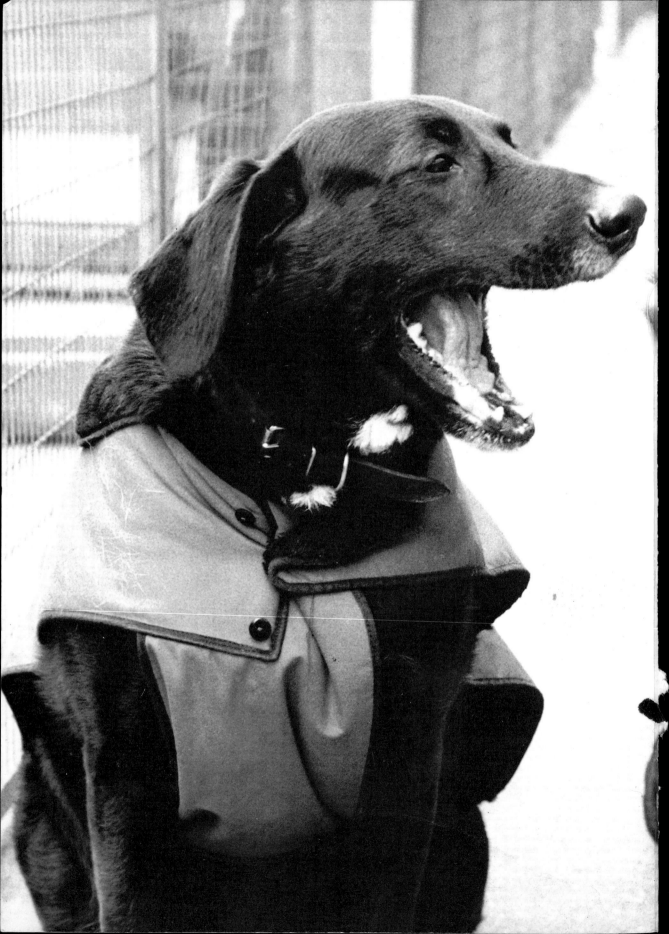